Becoming a Man After God's Own Heart

A LENTEN JOURNEY FOR MEN

BY STEVE BOLLMAN

PARADISUS DEI

HELPING FAMILIES DISCOVER THE SUPERABUNDANCE OF GOD

A Publication of Paradisus Dei • www.paradisusdei.org

A Lenten Journey for Men

How appropriate for our minds to return to King David as we begin our Lenten journey. One thousand years before Christ, he anticipated the Lenten program of the Church: "Turn away from sin and be faithful to the Gospel." King David could anticipate the Lenten journey of the Church because he understood that at the heart of the journey was an encounter with the merciful Father. King David understood mercy because King David needed mercy. He was chosen by God to be the leader of Israel. He was blessed by God with great wealth and power. He was confronted by God for his grievous sin: adultery and accomplish to murder. He was embraced by God for his sincere repentance: "Create in me a clean heart, O God, and put a new and right spirit within me. Cast me not away from thy presence, and take not thy holy Spirit from me. Restore to me the joy of thy salvation and uphold me with a willing spirit" *(Psalm 51:10ff)*.

There is a bit of King David in each of us. Although we are not Kings, we must admit that we have been highly blessed by God. Whatever our personal sins, we must admit that they are offensive in the eyes of God. However far we have fallen, we must admit that God's mercy is greater: "Have I any pleasure in the death of the wicked, says the Lord God, and not rather that he should turn from his way and live?" *(Ezekiel 18:23)*.

Our Lenten journey is not so much about where we have been. Rather, it is about where we are going. We are on journey to an encounter with the Father "who is rich in mercy" *(Ephesians 2:4)*. We trust that although we may still be a great distance away, he will hasten to encounter us and lead us home *(Cf. Luke 15:20)*. He will restore to us the dignity of the sons of God *(Cf. Luke 15:22ff)*. We will enter into his house and there will be great rejoicing *(Cf. Luke 15:24ff)*.

To aid in our journey, a Lenten program has been organized according to the days and the weeks of Lent. The "forty days of Lent" are calculated as the days from Ash Wednesday to Holy Saturday excluding Sundays. These forty days fall across 6½ weeks: Week of Ash Wednesday (½ week); First Week of Lent; Second Week of Lent; Third Week of Lent; Fourth Week of Lent; Fifth Week of Lent; and Holy Week.

THE FORTY DAYS OF LENT

Each day of Lent has four practices intended to help us attain "a personal encounter with Jesus Christ so that Jesus Christ can transform our lives."

Morning Consecration: Each morning we consecrate ourselves and our day to God. We will trust more in his goodness than in our own prudence.

Daily Exercise: Each day during Lent we should spend 15 minutes on our Lenten exercises which are designed to help us overcome the obstacles in the spiritual life and encounter the living God.

Daily Sacrifice or Offering: Each day during Lent we should make the sacrifice or offering indicated which are designed to compliment the spiritual exercise.

Night Prayer: We close our day by briefly considering how faithful we have been to our Lenten exercises and then expressing confidence in the Lord's grace and mercy.

THE WEEKS OF LENT

Counting the week of Ash Wednesday, there are seven weeks of Lent. Each of these weeks of Lent has four organizing principles.

Orientation: Each of the three fundamental orientations of the human person—towards self, towards others and toward God – is considered twice during the Lenten journey. First is considered how Satan attempts to distort these orientations, then how God seeks to encounter us through these orientations. Holy Week is dedicated to the mercy of God.

Exercise: Each week has an exercise (to be performed daily) that helps the soul to either withstand temptation or to encounter God according to the appropriate weekly orientation.

Sacrifice or Offering: Each week has a sacrifice or offering (to be performed daily) designed to reinforce the weekly exercise. These sacrifices allow our Lenten program to bear fruit.

Covenant: During the course of the Lenten journey, the Seven Covenants of That Man is You! will be developed. Each week will be dedicated to one covenant. ▪

The Three Fundamental Orientations of Man

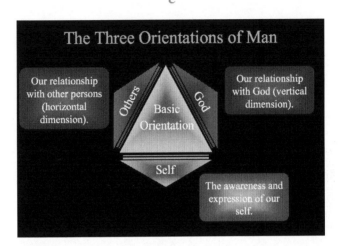

The Three Orientations of Man

Our relationship with other persons (horizontal dimension).

Our relationship with God (vertical dimension).

Others

God

Basic Orientation

Self

The awareness and expression of our self.

Every man has three fundamental orientations. Not more. Not less. These three orientations are so comprehensive that they transcend this world to touch the next. These three orientations fully define your life. They are your orientation towards yourself. Your orientation towards other people. And your orientation towards God.

THE ORIENTATION TOWARDS SELF
The most basic of the three fundamental orientations is the awareness of self. Indeed, one of the earliest developmental stages of the human brain is the ability to distinguish itself from every other thing. The perception that we form of ourselves will then directly influence the manner in which we will interact with other people and with God. The orientation towards self is critical to the spiritual life: "Love your neighbor as yourself" *(Cf. Matthew 19:19)*.

THE ORIENTATION TOWARDS OTHERS
The second fundamental orientation is towards other people. This orientation is often considered the "horizontal orientation" and changes throughout our life: from our family of origin, to our friends, to our spouse and children, to the larger world. The orientation towards other people is critical to the spiritual life: "He who does not love his brother whom he has seen, cannot love God whom he has not seen" *(1 John 4:20)*.

THE ORIENTATION TOWARDS GOD
The final and ultimate orientation of the human person is towards God. We have come from God and we are going to God. He is our "alpha and omega" *(Revelation 21:6)*. The distinguishing characteristic of man is that he is not limited to the boundaries of this world, but that his soul soars to seek union with the transcendent God. Therefore, each of the other orientations must open to an encounter with God: "As a hart longs for flowing streams, so longs my soul for thee, O God. My soul thirsts for God, for the living God" *(Psalm 42:1)*. ▪

The Three Exercises of Becoming a Man After God's Own Heart

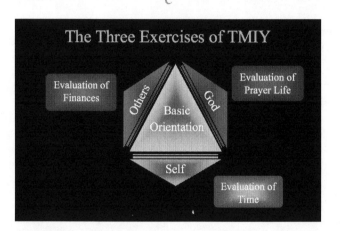

An honest evaluation of the current state of one's spiritual life is the necessary prerequisite to launch out on the path of transformation. This evaluation should consider each of man's three fundamental orientations. To help men make an objective evaluation, That Man is You! has developed three exercises, one exercise suited to each orientation.

THE EVALUATION OF TIME

Time is the surest measure of the orientation towards self. Time ultimately belongs to God: "Christ, yesterday and today, the beginning and the end. Alpha and Omega. All time belongs to him" *(Easter Vigil)*. All of us have received a set amount of time from God. None of us knows how much. How we spend our time is how we spend ourselves. The exercise on the evaluation of time helps each man obtain an objective understanding of how he spends his time; towards self, towards others and towards God. It then provides a vision of a balanced orientation towards self.

THE EVALUATION OF FINANCES

Each time that we make or spend a dollar we interact with another person. As such, the manner in which we handle our finances becomes an objective standard about how we interact with other people. The exercise on the evaluation of finances helps men obtain an objective understanding of the way in which we use money; towards self, towards others and towards God. It then provides a vision for a balanced approach to the use of money and the things of this world.

THE EVALUATION OF PRAYER

The ultimate orientation of the human person is towards God. Prayer allows us to enter into communion with God—even today. As such, prayer is the surest means for understanding our orientation towards God. We are called to dedicate an appropriate amount of time to God daily and to encounter him both individually and together with other people. The exercise for the evaluation of prayer helps men objectively understand their prayer lives and sets forth the vision of a balanced orientation towards God. ∎

The Three Fundamental Temptations in the Spiritual Life

❧

"All that is in the world, the concupiscence of the flesh, the concupiscence of the eyes and the pride of life, is not of the Father but is of the world." *(1 John 2:16)*

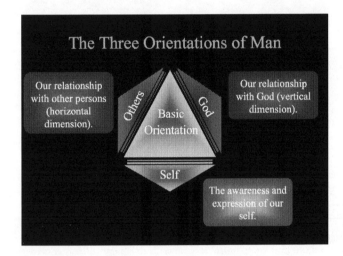

Before Christ began his public ministry he was led into the desert where he was tempted by the devil. Since Christ is "the man" *(John 19:5)*, his temptation in the desert reveals the temptations to which every man is submitted. The first temptation relates to the demands of the flesh: "If you are the Son of God, command this stone to become bread" *(Luke 4:3)*. The second temptation relates to the desire to rule over others: "The devil took him up, and showed him all the kingdoms of the world in a moment of time, and said to him, 'To you I will give all this authority and their glory; for it has been delivered to me, and I give it to whom I will. If you, then, will worship me, it shall all be yours'" *(Luke 4:5ff)*. The final temptation is against God, whom the devil has vowed to oppose: "[The devil] took him to Jerusalem, and set him on the pinnacle of the temple, and said to him, 'If you are the Son of God, throw yourself down from here; for it is written, 'He will give his angels charge of you, to guard you,' and 'On their hands they will bear you up, lest you strike your foot against a stone'"" *(Luke 4:9ff)*.

It is not coincidental that these three temptations, the flesh, the world and the devil, relate to the three fundamental orientations of the human person. These three temptations are a distortion of man's fundamental orientations. The temptation of the flesh is a distortion of the orientation towards self. The temptation of the world is a distortion of the orientation towards others. The temptation of the devil is a distortion of the orientation towards God.

THE TEMPTATION OF THE FLESH

The temptation of the flesh is the first of St. John's triple concupiscence. It is a distortion of the orientation towards self since it relates to the passions of the human heart. These passions are disordered when they set something above God. Historically, the disordered passions of the human heart have been categorized as the Seven Capital (or Deadly) Sins: pride, lust, greed, envy, anger, sloth and gluttony. These passions are so tightly bound together that when one becomes disordered, then they all become disordered; whenever progress is made against one, then progress is made against all.

THE TEMPTATION OF THE WORLD

The temptation of the world is the second of St. John's triple concupiscence. It is a distortion of the orientation towards other people since it is manifest in the desire to rule over others or in the objectification of others to satisfy one's own desires. "The world" becomes an obstacle in the spiritual life when someone sets the pursuit of the material goods of this world and the power and prestige that accompany them above the pursuit of God. Indeed, Scripture reveals the disordered love of money to be idolatry: "Put to death therefore what is earthly in you: immorality, impurity, passion, evil desire, and covetousness [greed], which is idolatry" *(Colossians 3:5)*.

THE TEMPTATION OF THE DEVIL

The pride of life is the final of St. John's triple concupiscence. It is a distortion of the orientation towards God and relates to the temptation of the devil since by it the devil attempts to ensnare us in his own rebellion against God. The devil fell when he declared his independence from God: "I will not serve" *(Jeremiah 2:20)*. When he did so, he set himself in opposition to God: "How are you fallen from heaven … you said I will ascend above the heights of the clouds; I will make myself like the Most High *(Isaiah 14:12ff)*. As such, the devil is the enemy of the soul's union with God: "Be sober, be watchful. Your adversary the devil prowls around like a roaring lion, seeking some one to devour" *(1 Peter 5:8)*. He tempts man to live independent of God. When man does so, he invariably accepts Satan's temptation to "become like god" *(Genesis 3:5)*. It is the ultimate expression of the pride of life. ■

The Pathway to an Encounter with the Living God

"That Man is You! is ultimately about a personal encounter with Jesus Christ so that Jesus Christ can transform you life." *(Steve Bollman, Founder, That Man is You! program)*

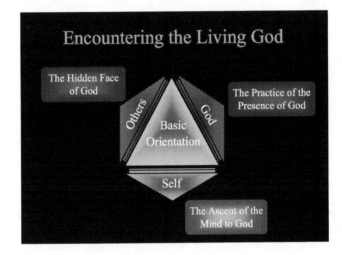

The beauty of Christianity is that our God comes to us! No other religion on earth has a God that humbled himself to share our very nature: "Though [Jesus Christ] was in the form of God, [he] did not count equality with God a thing to be grasped, but emptied himself, taking the form of a servant, being born in the likeness of men" *(Philippians 2:6ff)*. Jesus Christ continues to come to us today. He seeks to encounter us according to each of our orientations. He seeks to immerse us in an encounter with our God: "[God] is not far from each one of us, for 'In him we live and move and have our being'" *(Acts 17:27ff)*. The goal in the spiritual life is to open ourselves to an encounter with God according to each of our fundamental orientations. To aid men in this endeavor, That Man is You! has three spiritual practices, one suited to each fundamental orientation.

THE ASCENT OF THE MIND TO GOD

Jesus Christ abides in the Scriptures: "You search the Scriptures, because you think that in them you have eternal life; and it is they that bear witness to me" *(John 5:39)*. Jesus Christ wishes to speak to you personally through the Scriptures. However, since God speaks in "a still, small voice" *(1 Kings 19:12)*, we must quiet the distractions of our mind and attune them to the voice of God. The Ascent of the Mind to God utilizes Lectio Divina to discover the voice of Christ speaking through the Scriptures. We read passages of Scripture slowly, lingering when something strikes us. We meditate on the passage asking, "What is God saying to ME through the passage?" We pray that God will "open-up" the passage for us. We listen for the still, small voice of God. When we hear it, the Scriptures become the joy of our heart: "When I found your words, I devoured them; they became my joy and the happiness of my heart" *(Jeremiah 15:16)*.

THE HIDDEN FACE OF GOD

Jesus Christ abides in every human soul: "We are the temple of the living God" *(2 Corinthians 6:16)*. Therefore, each and every time that you encounter another person, you encounter God dwelling in that person. This is especially true between spouses who receive a special grace in the Sacrament of Marriage. Bridegroom and bride seal their marriage in the name of God: "Shelly, receive this ring as a sign of my love and fidelity. In the name of the Father. And of the Son. And of the Holy Spirit. Amen." Since Christ promised that "where two or three are gathered in my name, there am I in the midst of them" *(Matthew 18:20)*, he abides in the midst of the spousal union by definition. Each time that you encounter your spouse, you encounter God abiding in her. Concealed behind every encounter with your spouse is the Hidden Face of God. To experience his presence you must trust in and unpack the grace of the Sacrament of Marriage. If you truly desire, Christ will reveal himself through your spouse. You will see his "comely face and hear his sweet voice" *(Song of Solomon 2:14)* and your home will be transformed into a type of Paradise.

THE PRACTICE OF THE PRESENCE OF GOD

Jesus Christ dwells within every human soul: "If a man loves me, he will keep my word, and my Father will love him, and we will come to him and make our home with him" *(John 14:23)*. The most powerful practice in the spiritual life is to simply become aware of and unite yourself to Christ's abiding presence within. The Practice of the Presence of God seeks to facilitate just such an encounter. The Practice of the Presence of God is the simplest practice in the spiritual life: wherever you are and whatever you are doing, unite yourself to Christ. When you find that you're not united to Christ, simply unite yourself at that moment. The Practice of the Presence of God is intimately united to the Eucharist. Our goal is simply to perpetuate throughout our day and throughout our lives that moment when the Eucharistic Christ profoundly enters our souls. The Practice of the Presence of God is the sweetest practice in the spiritual life: when you encounter Christ within, you receive a foretaste of a joy that "no eye has seen, nor ear heard, nor heart of man conceived" *(1 Corinthians 2:9)*. ▩

Orientation: Self

Exercise: Time Evaluation

Sacrifice: Favorite Food

Covenant: Sexual Purity

"Let us conduct ourselves becomingly as in the day, not in reveling and drunkenness, not in debauchery and licentiousness, not in quarreling and jealousy. But put on the Lord Jesus Christ, and make no provision for the flesh, to gratify its desires."
(Romans 13:13-14)

ORIENTATION: Self. The most fundamental orientation of the human person is towards self. One of the first actions of a developing infant's brain is to distinguish itself from everything else. This self-awareness will determine the individual's interaction with the world and, ultimately, with God. An objective understanding of our orientation towards self is the starting point for our Lenten journey.

DAILY EXERCISE: The evaluation of time. Time is the surest measure of the orientation towards self. All of us have received a set amount of time from God. None of us knows how much. How we spend our time is how we spend ourselves. If we spend a disordered amount of time on our own pursuits, our lives will be characterized by selfishness, which is manifest through the Seven Capital Sins (pride, lust, greed, envy, anger, sloth and gluttony).

DAILY SACRIFICE: Favorite food or drink. The means for rightly ordering our orientation towards self is penance. Since sex and food/drink are the two most sensual pleasures, they are most frequently disordered at the same time. Therefore, a sure means of helping control the tendency to lust is to control the consumption of food and drink.

COVENANT: Sexual Purity. A balanced orientation towards self is dependent upon rightly ordered passions: pride, lust, greed, envy, anger, sloth and gluttony. The temptation to lust is particularly strong for men in modern culture. Make progress in relating to the temptation to lust and you will make progress against all your passions.

The Orientation Towards Self

First Lenten Exercise: Analysis of Time

"Christ, yesterday and today, the beginning and the end. Alpha and Omega. All time belongs to him." *(Easter Vigil)*

PRINCIPLES

Time is a gift from God. Therefore, God receives the first fruits (ten percent) of our time— 2.5 hours/day.

"It is not good for man to be alone" *(Genesis 2:18)*. We should spend twice as much time with others as we do by ourselves.

"Therefore a man leaves his father and his mother and cleaves to his wife and they become one flesh" *(Genesis 2:24)*. The fundamental communion is the family. We should spend three times as much time with our family as we do with others.

EXERCISE: ANALYSIS OF TIME

- Gather detailed records of the use of your time for one week.
- Be specific. Note what you were doing while driving. Note whether lunch was alone or with others; whether it was business or social, etc.
- Categorize the use of your time according to the three fundamental orientations as indicated on the accompanying worksheet.
- Work hours should be calculated exclusive of transportation to and from work and lunches during the day, which are considered separately.
- Lunches during the day are calculated as work time if it is a "working lunch," social time with others if taken with work associates (without working) and personal time if taken alone.
- Unless transportation time is specifically used otherwise (i.e. prayer/business/social) it should be considered as personal time.
- Absolute certainty regarding the categorization of time is not as important as an accurate picture of how our time was spent.
- Note the variance between personal use of time and a balanced orientation.
- Determine two specific steps to be taken to live a more balanced orientation.

ORIENTATION	ACTUAL	BALANCED	DIFFERENCE
TOWARDS GOD			
Mass	45		
Scripture Reading			
Private Prayer	15		
Family Prayer	20		
Other Spiritual (including TMIY)	30		
Total Time Spent towards God		2.5	
TOWARDS OTHERS			
Towards Spouse		1.0	
Household logistics			
Discussing children/household			
Meals with spouse alone			
Private time with spouse alone Teats			
Towards Children		2.0	
Helping with homework			
Activities (including transportation)			
Basic chores			
Entertainment (excluding TV)			
Other			
Towards Others		1.0	
Social			
Sports related			
Work Associates			
Other			
Total Time Spent towards Others		4.0	
TOWARDS SELF			
Work Related		8.0	
Work at Job	7.5		
Work at Home			
Working Lunch			
Required Entertainment			
Other			
Personal		2.0	
Meals by self			
Media by self (TV, Internet, music, etc.)			
Reading			
Household activities by self			
Transportation by self			
Other			
Sleep		7.0	
Personal Hygiene		0.5	
Total Time Spent towards Self		17.5	
TOTAL TIME		24.0	

The Covenant on Sexual Purity

"I will live in sexual purity according to the sixth and ninth commandments
and I will take whatever action is necessary to safeguard sexual purity for myself,
my spouse and my children."

FREEDOM. The first three covenants of TMIY are designed to give men freedom. Christ
promised to set his disciples free: "If you continue in my word, you are truly my disciples, and
you will know the truth, and the truth will make you free" *(John 8:32)*. The freedom which
he promised was the freedom from sin: "He who sins is the slave of sin" *(John 8:34)*. St. John
identified the tendency to sin as the triple concupiscence: "the concupiscence of the flesh, the
concupiscence of the eyes and the pride of life" *(1 John 2:16)*. The concupiscence of the flesh
includes all the passions or Seven Capital Sins: Pride, Lust, Greed, Envy, Anger, Sloth and
Gluttony. These passions are present in every person. When one increases, they all increase.
When progress is made against one, progress is made against all.

The first covenant of TMIY is designed to give men freedom from the interior passions by
tackling the temptation to lust, which is a particular problem for men in our culture. The
consumption of pornography has exploded. It is striking at the heart of authentic fatherhood.
It is striking at the heart of the family. King David struggled with the sin of lust. It wrecked
havoc with David, his family and his kingdom. Eventually, he overcame it to become
"a man after God's own heart" *(Acts 13:22)*. God wishes to give you the grace to overcome
the temptation to lust.

There are seven steps to obtaining sexual purity:

- Enter into a relationship with Christ in the Eucharist and ask for the grace
  to see women as he saw his mother at the foot of the Cross.
- Remove yourself from temptations against purity.
- Moderate your consumption of alcohol and food.
- When looking at a woman, focus on her face.
- Encounter women as persons by talking about their families.
- Never publicly speak ill about your spouse or participate in derogatory
  conversations about women.
- Whenever you've fallen, go to confession.

Orientation: Others

Exercise: Financial Evaluation

Sacrifice: Charity

Covenant: Financial Responsibility

"Do not love the world or the things in the world. If any one loves the world, love for the Father is not in him. For all that is in the world, the lust of the flesh and the lust of the eyes and the pride of life, is not of the Father but is of the world. And the world passes away, and the lust of it; but he who does the will of God abides for ever." *(1 John 2:15-17)*

ORIENTATION: Others. The second fundamental orientation of the human person is towards other people. The most important relationship we have with other people is with our family. As a child, it is with our parents and siblings. As an adult, it is with our spouse and children. An understanding of these relationships is essential to an understanding of our spiritual lives.

DAILY EXERCISE: The evaluation of finances. Each time that we make or spend a dollar we interact with another person. As such, the manner in which we handle our finances becomes an objective standard about how we interact with "the world." A disordered desire to accumulate wealth or material possessions (greed) will be manifest in a disordered relationship with other people and with God.

DAILY SACRIFICE: Charity. The means for rightly ordering our orientation towards others is charity. Instead of accumulating money for ourselves, we give it away. An excellent means of practicing charity during Lent is to voluntarily forgo something we enjoy and then give the money we would have spent to charity. An alternative is to use the money for debt reduction, which is a means of charity to the family.

COVENANT: Financial Responsibility. The greatest aid to achieving a balanced orientation towards others (and the world) is to use your financial resources responsibly. True financial freedom is attained when we understand that our material resources are called to be ordered towards God, then towards others and finally towards our self.

The Orientation towards Others

Second Lenten Exercise: Analysis of Finances

"**Where your treasure is, there will your heart also be.**" *(Matthew 6:21)*

PRINCIPLES

All of our financial resources are a gift or a blessing from God. Therefore, God receives the first fruits (ten percent) of our labor.

Since "the love of money is the root of all evil" *(1 Timothy 6:10)*, we should be very cautious in the pursuit and acquisition of material possessions.

Our financial resources are called to be used for the benefit of others. First, we are to provide for our families. Second, we are to save money so that we may provide for our children's future: "A good man leaves an inheritance to his children's children" *(Proverbs 13:22)*. Third, we are to practice charity to those in need: "Give to him who begs from you, and do not refuse him who would borrow from you" *(Matthew 5:42)*.

EXERCISE: ANALYSIS OF FINANCES

- Gather detailed records relating to your financial expenditures and debt.
- Convert all expenditures to a percentage of your BEFORE TAX earnings.
- Categorize your expenditures according to the three fundamental orientations as indicated on the accompanying worksheet.
- Include in the orientation towards God all TAX DEDUCTIBLE contributions: religious, education, medical, civic, etc.
- Include in the orientation towards others all savings and all gifts made to others that are not tax deductible.
- Be diligent in the accumulation of entertainment expenses. Include both those at home and those away from home.
- Meals eaten out should be included with entertainment expenses unless there was an identifiable alternative reason (i.e. business lunch).
- Calculate debt as a percentage of BEFORE TAX annual income.
- Calculate debt service (interest) as a percentage of BEFORE TAX annual income.
- Debt service for housing should include principle, interest, taxes and insurance.
- Note the variance between actual expenditures and a balanced orientation.
- If debt percentages are high, note the percentage of expenditures on entertainment.
- Determine two specific steps to be taken to attain a more balanced orientation.

SECOND LENTEN EXERCISE: ANALYSIS OF FINANCES

ORIENTATION	ACTUAL	BALANCED	DIFFERENCE
TOWARDS GOD			
Church/Religious Donations			
Educational Donations			
Civic Donations			
Finances directed towards God		10%	
TOWARDS OTHERS			
Savings			
Retirement			
Children's Education			
General			
Charity			
Parents			
Extended Family			
Others			
Finances directed towards Others		15%	
ENTERTAINMENT EXPENSES			
Internet/Satellite/Cable			
Meals with family			
Meals with friends			
Lunch/Happy Hour/Sports			
Entertaining			
Travel			
Other			
Finances directed towards Entertainment		5%	
DEBT ANALYSIS			
Debt			
Housing			
Automobiles			
Consumer			
Credit Card			
Other			
Debt Service (Interest on Debt)			
Housing (PITI)			
Automobiles			
Consumer			
Credit Card			
Other			
Debt Ratios			
Debt Service/Finances to God		< 2.5:1	
Debt Service/Finances to Others		< 1.7:1	
Debt Service/(Finances to God/Others)		< 1:1	

16

The Covenant on Financial Responsibility

"I will become financially responsible for myself and my family by giving God the first fruits of my labor, saving a portion of my earnings and eliminating all credit card debt."

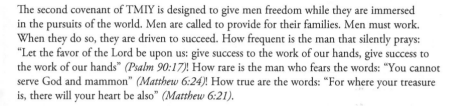

The second covenant of TMIY is designed to give men freedom while they are immersed in the pursuits of the world. Men are called to provide for their families. Men must work. When they do so, they are driven to succeed. How frequent is the man that silently prays: "Let the favor of the Lord be upon us: give success to the work of our hands, give success to the work of our hands" *(Psalm 90:17)*! How rare is the man who fears the words: "You cannot serve God and mammon" *(Matthew 6:24)*! How true are the words: "For where your treasure is, there will your heart be also" *(Matthew 6:21)*.

Satan distorts man's drive to succeed to ensnare him in the second of St. John's triple concupiscence: the world. Signs of greed, the desire to gain money and material possessions beyond reason, are present in abundance in our culture: excessive executive pay; the absence of charitable contributions; the lack of savings and the accumulation of debt. The second covenant of TMIY provides men freedom by rightly ordering man's pursuits in the world. They must be ordered to God, to family and to the individual.

There are seven steps to obtaining financial freedom and rightly ordering our orientation towards the world:

- Give the first fruits (ten percent) of your labor to God.
- Cut up all credit cards until they are paid off.
- Begin saving and gradually increase the amount.
- Live below your means.
- Cut entertainment expense by eating meals together at home and enjoying nature as recreation.
- Keep $8 in your wallet that you MUST give away.
- Moderate your consumption of the media.

Orientation: God

Exercise: Evaluation of Prayer

Sacrifice: Prayer

Covenant: Reclaiming the Sabbath

"Begone, Satan! for it is written, 'You shall worship the Lord your God and him only shall you serve.'" *(Matthew 4:10)*

ORIENTATION: God. The ultimate orientation of the human person is towards God. We have come from God and we are going to God. He is our alpha and omega. Each of our other orientations should find their fulfillment in the orientation towards God.

DAILY EXERCISE: Evaluation of Prayer Life. Prayer is simply communication with God. As such, an evaluation of our prayer life is the surest means for understanding our orientation towards God. We are called to dedicate an appropriate amount of time to God daily and to encounter him both individually and together with other people. A failure to do so will lead to a disordered relationship with God that is characterized by pride—the attempt to live independent of God.

DAILY SACRIFICE: Prayer. The means for rightly ordering our relationship with God is prayer. We should begin each day by considering where we are in need of God's grace: in our personal lives, in our families, in our communities and country. We should then humbly ask for God's guidance. We should end each day by considering where we have received the blessings of God and then thanking him.

COVENANT: Reclaiming the Sabbath. Satan is the ultimate enemy of the soul: "The devil prowls around like a roaring lion, seeking some one to devour" *(1 Peter 5:8)*. The surest means to overcome the temptations of Satan is to unite yourself to God. From the beginning, God established the Sabbath as the day that man could be united with God. Reclaim the Sabbath for God and you will be able to overcome the snares of the devil.

The Orientation Towards God

Third Lenten Exercise: Analysis of Prayer

"One thing have I asked of the Lord, that will I seek after; that I may dwell in the house of the Lord all the days of my life, to behold the beauty of the Lord and to inquire in his temple." *(Psalm 27:4)*

PRINCIPLES

OUR GOD COMES TO US! Jesus is "the living bread which came down from heaven" *(John 6:51)*. We should encounter Jesus in the Eucharist frequently and devoutly be attending Mass and embracing Eucharistic adoration.

Jesus Christ encounters us through the Scriptures: "You search the Scriptures, because you think that in them you have eternal life; and it is they that bear witness to me" *(John 5:39)*. The Scriptures are called to become "the delight of our heart" *(Jeremiah 15:16)*.

Jesus Christ comes to us through other people: "As you did it to one of the least of these my brethren, you did it to me" *(Matthew 25:40)*. He is present whenever "two or three are gathered in my name" *(Matthew 18:20)*.

EXERCISE: ANALYSIS OF PRAYER

- Gather detailed records relating to your time spent in prayer and spiritual activities.
- Categorize your prayer life and spiritual activities according to the three fundamental orientations as indicated on the accompanying worksheet.
- Note the variance between actual time devoted to prayer and a balanced orientation.
- Both the quantity of prayer time and its distribution between the three fundamental orientations are essential.
- A substantially reduced amount of time dedicated to prayer indicates someone who is living their life independent of God on the practical level.
- A prayer life composed almost exclusively of Mass frequently indicates an "institutional" relationship with God. It frequently indicates a "cultural Catholicism."
- A prayer life composed almost exclusively of prayer with other persons frequently tends towards a "social Christianity."
- A prayer life dedicated almost exclusively to the service of those in need runs the risk of falling into purely "social service" unless it is accompanied by a strong interior prayer life.
- A prayer life composed almost exclusively of personal prayer runs the risk of turning into "private devotion." Christ founded a community—the Church.
- Determine two specific steps to be taken to attain a more balanced orientation.

THIRD LENTEN EXERCISE: ANALYSIS OF PRAYER

ORIENTATION	ACTUAL	BALANCED	DIFFERENCE
TOWARDS GOD			
Mass			
Eucharistic Adoration			
Total Time Spent towards God		0.5 - 1.0	
TOWARDS OTHERS			
Prayer with Spouse			
Reading Scripture			
Rosary			
Other			
Prayer with Family			
Reading Scripture			
Rosary			
Other			
Prayer with Others			
Reading Scripture			
Rosary			
That Man is You!			
Service to those in need			
Other			
Total Time Spent towards Others		0.5 - 1.0	
TOWARDS SELF			
Reading Scripture			
Private Study			
Private Prayer			
Other			
Total Time Spent towards Self		0.5 - 1.5	
TOTAL TIME		2.5	

The Covenant on Reclaiming the Sabbath

"I will reclaim Sunday as the Lord's Day by attending Mass together
with my family and making the gift of that day to my family so that we may
experience the superabundant joy of God together."

⚜

The third covenant of TMIY is designed to help men overcome the snares of the devil by binding them more closely to God. Ultimately, all of Satan's temptations are an attempt to ensnare men in his own rebellion against God. Satan declared his independence from God: "I will not serve" *(Jeremiah 2:20)*. He then set himself in opposition to God: "How are you fallen from heaven ... you said, 'I will ascend above the heights of the clouds: I will make myself like the Most High'" *(Isaiah 14:12ff)*. Satan tempts men to live independent of God. He tempts them to make themselves into god.

Signs of man's attempt to live independent of God abound in our modern culture: few Catholics take the time to read Scripture, the living word of God; respect for man, created in the image and likeness of God, is missing; attendance at weekly worship services has decreased. Indeed, a significant portion of persons living in "western society" proclaim that God has no importance in their life.

From the beginning God intended the Sabbath to be the day that man was united with God: "Remember the Sabbath day, to keep it holy. Six days you shall labor, and do all your work, but the seventh day is a Sabbath to the Lord your God" *(Exodus 20:8)*. The Sabbath rest was designed to give man freedom: "Observe the Sabbath day ... remember that you were a servant in the land of Egypt, and the Lord your God brought you out ... therefore the Lord your God commanded you to keep the Sabbath day" *(Deuteronomy 5:12ff)*.

The temptation of Satan leads to slavery. The worship of God leads to freedom: the freedom from the anxieties of the world; the freedom of rest and leisure; the freedom to enjoy family and friends; the freedom to bask in the glory of the sons of God.

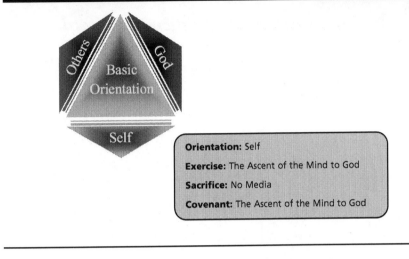

Orientation: Self

Exercise: The Ascent of the Mind to God

Sacrifice: No Media

Covenant: The Ascent of the Mind to God

"Thy word is a lamp to my feet and a light to my path. I have sworn an oath and confirmed it, to observe thy righteous ordinances." *(Psalm 119:105-106)*

ORIENTATION: Self. God "is not far from each one of us, for 'In him we live and move and have our being'" *(Acts 17:27-28)*. By reading Scripture we attune our minds to God so that we may discover his presence in our lives. Scripture is the living word of God. Through it God wishes to speak to you personally and reveal to you the mystery of your life.

DAILY EXERCISE: The Ascent of the Mind to God. Spend 15 minutes each day reading Scripture in silence. Practice Lectio Divina by reading slowing and pausing whenever something strikes you. Allow God to speak. Ensure that you are guided by the Church by reading authoritative Church teachings (such as the Catechism) and the writings of the saints.

DAILY SACRIFICE: No Media. God wishes to speak to you, but he speaks in a "still, small voice" *(Cf. 1 Kings 19:12)*. The noise of this world easily obscures the voice of God. If you wish to hear the voice of God, turn down the persistent clutter of the media. It will also help you "find the time" to read the Scriptures.

COVENANT: The Ascent of the Mind to God. Jesus Christ abides within the Scriptures. He wishes to speak to you personally through the Scriptures. If you wish to hear his voice, practice Lectio Divina while reading Scriptures 15 minutes each day.

The Orientation Towards Self

Lenten Practice: The Ascent of the Mind to God

"When I found your words, I devoured them; they became my joy and the happiness of my heart." *(Jeremiah 15:16)*

The Scriptures are the living Word of God. Through them Jesus Christ wishes to speak to you personally. To hear his voice, you must read the Scriptures differently from any other book. You must allow the Scriptures to speak to you. The Church's time honored method for listening to the voice of Christ speaking through the Scriptures is called Lectio Divina. It is based on four principles: Reading, Meditation, Prayer and Contemplation.

READING
- Gently read a passage of Scripture.
- When a thought, word or passage strikes you, pause to dwell on it, repeating it slowly.
- When the passage has "dried up," move on to the next.

MEDITATION
- Dwell at leisure on a morsel of the text.
- Personalize the passage by asking, "What is God saying to ME through the passage?"
- Do not work hard, actively trying to "crack" the text.
- Listen and allow God to speak through the text.

PRAYER
- Allow the Word of God to move from the lips to the heart so that there is a desire for the text to be "opened up."
- Pray for God to open the text for you: "Lord, that I might see" *(Luke 18:41)*.
- Ultimately, it is the desire for communion with God.

CONTEMPLATION
- The soul experiences God "speaking" or being "poured into" the soul.
- The soul cannot "force" the response of God. A moment of contemplation is God's initiative that must be received as gift.
- The soul should linger as long as it perceives God's presence.

The Ascent of the Mind to God

Scriptural Passages for the Third Week of Lent

SUNDAY

READ *Matthew 5:1-11*
Meditation Starter: The pathway to the kingdom of God is different
from the pathway to success in the world.

MONDAY

READ *Matthew 5:13-16*
Meditation Starter: Your life is called to show forth the pathway to the kingdom of God.

TUESDAY

READ *Matthew 5:27-32*
Meditation Starter: We must purify our interior life if our actions are to be pure.

WEDNESDAY

READ *Matthew 6:19-24*
Meditation Starter: The world should lead us to God and not away from him.

THURSDAY

READ Matthew *7:15-23*
Meditation Starter: The devil will always try to block our pathway to God.

FRIDAY

READ Matthew *6:25-34*
Meditation Starter: God desires to bless us. We must simply receive his blessing.

SATURDAY

READ Matthew *7:24-28*
Meditation Starter: Union with God will sustain us through all the trials in life.

The Covenant on the Ascent of the Mind to God

**"I will elevate my mind to God by spending at least fifteen minutes each day
gently reading Scripture and allowing God to speak to me. I will validate my insights
through my spouse and/or my spiritual guide as appropriate."**

If the first three covenants of TMIY were about freedom, then the second three are about joy—the superabundant joy of experiencing an encounter with the living God. The fourth covenant of TMIY is designed to help men experience the joy of hearing the voice of the Lord speak to them personally through the Scriptures.

Jesus Christ is present in the Scriptures: "The scriptures bear witness to me" *(Cf. John 5:39)*. Therefore, the Scriptures are not dead. They are the living word of God: "The word of God is living and active, sharper than any two-edged sword, piercing to the division of soul and spirit, of joints and marrow, and discerning the thoughts and intentions of the heart" *(Hebrews 4:12)*.

Jesus Christ wishes to speak to you personally through the Scriptures! However, the Lord of the universe does not shout. He whispers. He speaks in a "still small voice" *(Cf. 1 Kings 19:12)*. To hear his voice we must still the passions of the heart, silence the noise of the world and trust in the God who is meek and humble of heart: "Speak Lord, for your servant is listening" *(1 Samuel 3:10)*.

God will speak. He has spoken to countless men and women through the Scriptures and transformed their lives. Many are counted among the great saints of the Church. When you hear his "sweet voice" *(Song of Solomon 2:14)*, the Scriptures will become the joy of your heart: "When I found your words, I devoured them; they became my joy and the happiness of my heart" *(Jeremiah 15:16)*.

> **Orientation:** God
>
> **Exercise:** The Practice of the Presence of God
>
> **Sacrifice:** Daily Visit to Christ in the Eucharist
>
> **Covenant:** The Practice of the Presence of God

"One thing have I asked of the Lord, that will I seek after; that I may dwell in the house of the Lord all the days of my life, to behold the beauty of the Lord, and to inquire in his temple." *(Psalm 27:5)*

ORIENTATION: God. Christianity is unique among all religions. We are not called to grope after God in hopes that we will find him *(Cf. Acts 17:27)*. Our God comes to us! He is Emmanuel: "God with us" *(Matthew 1:23)*. Christ came to us two thousand years ago as a little baby. He continues to come to us each day in the Eucharist. We must simply open ourselves to an encounter with our God.

DAILY EXERCISE: The Practice of the Presence of God. God dwells within each human soul. The simplest, yet most profound practice in the spiritual life is to become aware of God's abiding presence within the soul. Select something that you do repetitively throughout the day such as entering or leaving your office. Each time you do your selected action say a brief prayer, such as: "In him we live and move and have our being" *(Acts 17:28)*.

DAILY SACRIFICE: Daily visit to Christ in the Eucharist. The greatest aid to the Practice of the Presence of God is the frequent and devout reception of the Holy Eucharist. Receive the Eucharist as frequently as possible this week. When it is not possible, at least briefly visit the Eucharistic Jesus abiding in the Tabernacle.

COVENANT: The Practice of the Presence of God. God dwells within your soul. When you were baptized you became the "temple of the living God" *(2 Corinthians 6:16)*. Each time you receive the Eucharist, Christ profoundly enters your soul. The simplest, yet most profound practice in the spiritual life is to simply unite yourself to Christ abiding within your soul. Wherever you are and whatever you are doing, unite yourself to Christ and you will experience a sweetness that is a foretaste of that joy which has no end.

The Orientation Towards God

Lenten Practice:
The Practice of the Presence of God

"If a man loves me, he will keep my word, and my Father will love him, and we will come to him and make our home with him." *(John 14:23)*

⤲

Christianity is unique from any other religion in the world. In Christianity man does not ascend to God, our God comes to us: "Though he was in the form of God, [Jesus] did not count equality with God a thing to be grasped, but emptied himself, taking the form of a servant and being born in the likeness of men" *(Philippians 2:6ff)*. Two thousand years ago, God entered human history when the Word became incarnate and was born as a little baby in Bethlehem. Christ has promised to remain with us until the end of time: "Behold, I am with you always, until to the end of the world" *(Cf. Matthew 28:20)*. The greatest challenge in the spiritual life is to be aware of Christ's abiding presence.

The Practice of the Presence of God seeks to discover Christ's abiding presence within the soul. This practice is the simplest, sweetest and most profound practice in the spiritual life.

THE SIMPLEST PRACTICE

There are no formal rules to the Practice of the Presence of God. The soul seeks to discover the presence of God wherever it is and whatever it is doing by simply turning inward to unite itself with God abiding within the soul. Nonetheless, there are certain exercises that are beneficial in helping the soul to attune itself to God abiding within. The greatest aid to the Practice of the Presence of God is the frequent and devout reception of Christ in the Eucharist. When we receive the Eucharist, Christ truly and properly speaking comes to us and dwells within our souls.

THE SWEETEST PRACTICE

Our ultimate destiny is God. When we reach our destiny we will experience a joy that "no eye has seen, nor ear heard, nor heart of man conceived" *(1 Corinthians 2:9)*. By discovering the abiding presence of God within, we receive a foretaste of that joy to come: "I receive [from the Practice of the Presence of God] greater sweetness and satisfaction than an infant receives from his mother's breast" *(Brother Lawrence of the Resurrection)*.

THE MOST PROFOUND PRACTICE

A momentary encounter with Christ has transformed the lives of countless men and women. To be immersed in God is nothing other than to be "transformed from glory unto glory into the image of the Son" *(Cf. 2 Corinthians 3:18)*.

The Practice of the Presence of God

Steps to Finding God within the Soul

ATTENDING MASS
- Arrive at Mass a few minutes early and ask for the grace to set aside all of the distractions of your mind during the Mass.
- Ask for the forgiveness of your sins during the Penitential Rite.
- Be attentive to the reading of the Word of God and select one passage to "take home from the Mass."
- During the Consecration—at the moment of elevation—profoundly unite yourself to Christ and say a prayer such as: "My Lord and my God" *(John 20:28)*, or "God, be merciful to me a sinner" *(Luke 18:13)*, or "Lord, I believe; help my unbelief!" *(Mark 9:24)*.
- After receiving the Eucharist, silently unite yourself to Christ dwelling within your soul.
- After Mass, spend a moment with Christ to thank him for the opportunity to receive him and ask for the grace to unite yourself to him abiding within your soul throughout the day.

EUCHARISTIC ADORATION
- As frequently as possible, especially when you were unable to attend Mass, visit the Eucharistic Christ abiding in the Tabernacle.
- Unite yourself to Christ.
- Spend some moments in silence so that Christ may speak to you.
- Ask for the grace to unite yourself to Christ abiding within your soul throughout the day.

THROUGHOUT THE DAY
- Select an action that you do repetitively throughout the day, such as walking in and out of your office at work, starting your car, etc.
- Each time that you perform the selected action, briefly unite yourself to God and say a prayer such as: "In him we live and move and have our being" *(Acts 17:28)*.

IN THE HOME
- Upon entering or exiting the home, unite yourself to God and say a brief prayer such as: ENTERING: "I rejoiced when I heard them say, 'Let us go to the house of the Lord'" *(Psalm 122:1)* or "Blessed are those who dwell in your house, O Lord" *(Psalm 84:5)*; EXITING: "One day in your house is better than a thousand elsewhere" *(Psalm 84:10)* or "How lovely is your dwelling place, O Lord of hosts" *(Psalm 84:1)*.

THE LINGERING PRESENCE OF GOD
- The awareness of the presence of God within the soul becomes more spontaneous and subtle.
- The soul is able to unite itself to God with ease whenever a momentary break in its activities occurs.
- No words need be spoken. There is a simple awareness of God's abiding presence within the soul.

The Covenant on the Practice of the Presence of God

"I will Practice the Presence of God by receiving Christ in the Eucharist one time each week in addition to Sunday. If I am unable to receive Him in the Eucharist, I will at least stop to visit Him residing in the Tabernacle."

☙❧

The sixth covenant of TMIY seeks to transform the spiritual life of every man by unlocking the grace contained in the greatest treasure of the Church, the REAL PRESENCE of Jesus Christ in the Blessed Eucharist. Jesus Christ promised that he would remain with us until the end of time: "I am with you always, until the end of time" *(Cf. Matthew 28:20).* Jesus Christ promised that he would abide within us: "If a man loves me, he will keep my word, and my Father will love him, and we will come to him and make our home with him" *(John 14:23).* Through the gift of the Eucharist, Jesus Christ has fulfilled both promises! Through the gift of the Eucharist, Jesus Christ abides with us today! Through the gift of the Eucharist, Jesus Christ profoundly abides within us!

The Practice of the Presence of God seeks to extend our Eucharistic encounter with Christ throughout our day, throughout our lives. We simply need to recollect ourselves and turn inward to find the abiding presence of Christ. Indeed the simplicity of the practice often obscures it profundity. Nonetheless, when we are able to easily unite ourselves to God dwelling within, our lives are transformed. We understand that we are living Tabernacles: "We are the temple of the living God" *(2 Corinthians 6:16).* And, if we are the Tabernacle of the living God, then we are being "transformed from glory unto glory into the image of the Son" *(Cf. 2 Corinthians 3:18).* Yes, in the Eucharist we become what we eat *(Cf. St. Pope Leo the Great, Sermon 12 on the Passion, #7).* It is truly the preparation for that joy that "no eye has seen, nor ear heard, nor heart of man conceived" *(1 Corinthians 2:9).* By the Practice of the Presence of God we receive—even today—a foretaste of that joy to come.

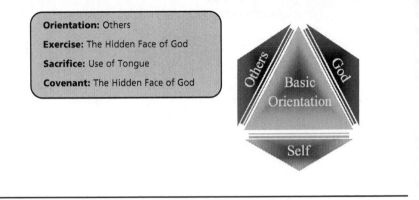

Orientation: Others

Exercise: The Hidden Face of God

Sacrifice: Use of Tongue

Covenant: The Hidden Face of God

"Seven times a day I praise thee for thy righteous ordinances." *(Psalm 119:164)*

ORIENTATION: Others. God encounters us through other people: "As you did it to one of the least of these my brethren, you did it to me" *(Matthew 25:40)*. This is especially true for spouses who seal their marriage in the name of God. Christ has promised: "Where two or three are gathered in my name, there am I in the midst of them" (Matthew 18:20). Each time that you encounter your spouse, you encounter God abiding in her!

DAILY EXERCISE: The Hidden Face of God. Each time you encounter your spouse or child, interiorly say the brief prayer: "Show me your face" *(Song of Solomon 2:14)*. Whenever you need guidance say the brief prayer, "Speak, for your servant is listening" *(1 Samuel 3:10)*, ask your spouse her opinion and trust that God has guided you through her.

DAILY SACRIFICE: Use of Tongue. Our tongue was made to praise God! Yet, "with it we bless the Lord and Father, and with it we curse men, who are made in the likeness of God. From the same mouth come blessing and cursing. My brethren, this ought not be so" *(James 3:9-10)*. During this week we will stop seven times during the day to thank God for all the blessings he has given us and we will not say one negative or harsh thing to our families.

COVENANT: Finding the Hidden Face of God. Christianity is an "incarnational" religion. Our God became visible to us in Jesus Christ "which we have heard, which we have seen with our eyes, which we have looked upon and touched with our hands" *(1 John 1:1)*. Jesus Christ still wishes to manifest himself today. However, now his face is hidden behind those whom you encounter. Seek the hidden face of Christ in your wife and children and your life will be forever changed.

The Orientation Towards Others
Lenten Practice: The Hidden Face of God

"We are the temple of the living God; as God said, 'I will live in them and move among them, and I will be their God, and they shall be my people.'" *(2 Corinthians 6:16)*

God dwells in every human soul. Therefore, each and every time that you encounter another person, you encounter God dwelling in that person. Each person you meet becomes for you the manifestation of the hidden face of God.

This is especially true between spouses who receive a special grace in the Sacrament of Matrimony. Bridegroom and bride seal their marriage in the name of God: "Shelly, receive this ring as a sign of my love and fidelity. In the name of the Father. And of the Son. And of the Holy Spirit. Amen." Since Christ promised that "where two or three are gathered in my name, there am I in the midst of them" *(Matthew 18:20)*, he abides in the midst of the spousal union by definition. Each time that you encounter your spouse, you encounter God abiding in her. She is for you in a very unique and personal way, the hidden face of God. To discover the hidden face of God ever more profoundly, interiorly say the following prayers when interacting with your spouse:

"Lord, show me your face" *(Song of Solomon 2:14)*.

"Speak, for your servant is listening" *(1 Samuel 3:10)*.

Discovering the hidden face of God is a source of tremendous joy in the spiritual life. We should spontaneously break into the praise of God: "Seven times a day I praise thee" *(Psalm 119:164)*.

The Hidden Face of God

Praise of God for the Fourth Week of Lent

(See inside back cover of booklet)

Praise Upon Rising

"O Lord God of hosts, how lovely is your dwelling place! One day within your courts is better than a thousand elsewhere. I would rather be a doorkeeper in the house of the Lord than to dwell in the tents of the wicked. Blessed are those who dwell in your house forever singing your praises."

Morning Praise

"O merciful Father, what is man that you should be mindful of him, mortal man that you should care for him? Yet to ransom a sinner you gave away your only beloved Son. How great is your name, O Lord our God, through all the earth!"

Midmorning Praise

"O beloved Son of the Father, in your light we see light. We behold the revelation of the Father, slow to anger and abiding in compassion. O Lord, your mercy is as high as the heavens and as deep as the nether world. How great is your name, O Lord our God, through all the earth!"

Midday Praise

"O Spirit of love, you transform us from glory unto glory into the image of the only begotten of the Father. What you reveal to us now dimly as in a mirror, you will one day reveal to us face to face. How great is your name, O Lord our God, through all the earth!"

Midafternoon Praise

"O mystery of life and love, how sweet the path of those who find you abiding in their homes, who gaze upon the beauty of your face and hear the sweet sound of your voice. Praise to you, Lord of heaven and earth, for you have hidden these things from the wise and learned and have revealed them to the pure of heart."

Evening Praise

"O Emmanuel! How great your love for those who serve you! How near your presence to those who love you! You dwell with those gathered in your name. Stay with us, Lord, for the day is far spent and evening presses. O Emmanuel, be ever near to us!"

Night Praise

"O gracious God, now you may let your servant go in peace for your word has been fulfilled; my own eyes have beheld your mercy that is from generation unto generation to those who love you. How great is your name, O Lord our God, through all the earth!"

The Covenant on Finding the Hidden Face of God

"I will stop what I am doing and praise God seven times each day for discovering his Hidden Face in those closest to me, especially in my wife and children."

Of the seven covenants in TMIY, the fifth is the most unique. In reality, it is the fruit of an action rather than the action itself. It is the expression of joy rather than the action leading to joy. The action is the discovery of the Hidden Face of God in those most dear to us, those most intimate to us, our family. Hidden within this simple practice is the power to profoundly transform our lives and those of our families.

How near is our God to us! How profoundly does he wish to manifest himself to us! To experience his presence we must unpack the grace of the Sacrament of Marriage. Jesus Christ promised: "where two or three are gathered in my name, there am I in the midst of them" *(Matthew 18:20)*. Bridegroom and bride seal their union in the name of God: "Shelly, receive this ring as a sign of my love and fidelity. In the name of the Father. And of the Son. And of the Holy Spirit. Amen." Jesus Christ is present in the midst of the spousal union by definition! Concealed behind every encounter with our spouse is the Hidden Face of God. How inexhaustible the graces of the Sacrament of Marriage!

When we pull back the veil of this mystery, we truly experience that "in God we live and move and have our being" *(Acts 17:28)*. Our families are transformed into a type of Paradise and we experience a joy that no one can take from us. It is this joy that bursts forth into a sacrifice of praise. Praise for the mercy God has shown us in immersing us in himself. Praise for Emmanuel—our God who is ever near us. Praise for our home and family where we encounter our God. "How great is your name, O Lord our God, through all the earth" *(Psalm 8:1)*.

Orientation: The Merciful Father

Exercise: Examination of Conscience

Sacrifice: Miserere (see inside front cover)

Covenant: The Mercy of God

"Have mercy on me, O God, according to thy great mercy; and according to the multitude of thy tender mercies blot out my iniquity. Wash me yet more from my iniquity, and cleanse me from my sin ... Create a clean heart in me, O God: and renew a right spirit within my bowels. Cast me not away from thy face; and take not thy holy spirit from me. Restore unto me the joy of thy salvation, and strengthen me with a perfect spirit." *(Psalm 51:1ff)*

ORIENTATION: The Merciful Father. Our entire Lenten journey is a preparation for an encounter with the Father "who is rich in mercy" *(Ephesians 2:4)*. As this encounter approaches, our eyes are fixed ever more intently upon him.

DAILY EXERCISE: Examination of Conscience. Each morning we will make an examination of conscience of our previous life against the objective standard of the Ten Commandments. An aid for the examination of conscience is provided. Sometime during Holy Week (or earlier if necessary) we will receive the mercy of God in the Sacrament of Reconciliation.

DAILY SACRIFICE: Miserere of David (see inside front cover). Standing at the moment of transformation between "That man is you!" *(2 Samuel 12:7)* and "A man after God's own heart" *(Acts 13:22)* is King David's repentance. It has been captured in Psalm 51. It is so important that the Church recites it every Friday of the year. We will recite it each day of Holy Week after making our examination of conscience.

COVENANT: The Mercy of God. That Man is You! is about a personal encounter with Jesus Christ so that Jesus Christ can transform your life. He wants to encounter you right where you are in your spiritual life and take you to a better place. Your sins cannot exhaust his mercy. Offer him your sins and he will offer you life, light, peace and joy.

The Orientation Towards Mercy

Lenten Exercise:
Receive and Practice the Mercy of God

Christ identified mercy as an ESSENTIAL characteristic of Christianity: "I desire mercy and not sacrifice" *(Matthew 9:13).* Indeed, we are called to receive the mercy of God and to practice the mercy of God: **"Be merciful, even as your Father is merciful"** *(Luke 6:36).*

RECEIVING THE MERCY OF GOD

When Christ wished to remain with us until the end of time, he gave us the Eucharist: "For my flesh is food indeed, and my blood is drink indeed" *(John 6:55).* When he wished to perpetuate the mercy flowing forth from Calvary, he gave us the gift of confession: "If you forgive the sins of any, they are forgiven; if you retain the sins of any, they are retained" *(John 20:23).* Christ makes his mercy present to us in the Sacrament of Reconciliation! A good confession includes four elements:

Examination of Conscience
We examine the state of our lives since our last confession against an objective moral standard such as the Ten Commandments. (An aid for the examination of conscience is provided on the following page.)

Contrition
The soul should have sorrow of the sins it has committed and the consequences of those sins. It should make a firm resolution not to sin again.

Confession
The soul should make an individual confession to a priest within the context of the Sacrament of Reconciliation.

Satisfaction
The soul should make satisfaction for its sins by fulfilling the "penance" given by the priest and making reparation for its sins as appropriate. Prudence should be exercised and the advice of a priest sought in acts of reparation.

PRACTICING THE MERCY OF GOD

The gifts that we have received, we are called to give *(Cf. Matthew 10:8).*
Experiencing the mercy of God, we must practice the mercy of God! We must do so as we have experienced it—superabundantly!

- We must willingly forgive those who have wronged us.
- We should help our family avoid sin and the occasions of sin.
- We should perform one gratuitous act for each member of our family every week.

The Reception of the Mercy of God

Examination of Conscience before Confession

I am the Lord your God.

You shall have no false gods before me.

Do I follow the teachings of the Church?

Do I devote sufficient time to prayer?

Do I support the Church financially?

Have I endangered my faith by reading, watching or listening to materials contrary to the faith and/or containing bad morals?

Do not take the Lord's name in vain.

Have I used the name of God, Christ, Our Lady, the saints or the Church without reverence?

Have I taken a false oath or committed perjury?

Keep holy the Sabbath.

Did I miss Mass on Sunday or a Holy Day of Obligation without a sufficiently grave reason?

Do I set aside my business and other activities that would inhibit the worship due to God and the rest and relaxation proper to the Lord's Day?

Honor your father and mother.

Did I neglect to help my parents when they were in need?

Do I treat my parents with little affection and/or respect?

Do I teach my children and help them live the Catholic faith by helping them avoid the temptations of the world?

Do not kill.

Have I ever taken a life with the exception of self-defense?

Have I had, performed or aided someone in procuring an abortion?

Have I led others into sin?

Have I spoken unjustly about another person and/or ruined another person's reputation?

Have I been unjustly harsh in disciplining my children?

Do not commit adultery.

Have I had sexual intercourse outside of the bonds of marriage?

Do I use contraception?

Do not steal.

Have I taken something that does not belong to me?

Have I failed to pay a just wage to my employees?

Do not bear false witness.

Have I told lies?

Do I engage in gossip?

Do not covet thy neighbor's wife.

Do I lust after women?

Do I look at pornography or watch movies with inappropriate sexual content?

Do I put myself into occasions of sin with other women?

Have I masturbated?

Do not covet thy neighbor's goods.

Am I envious of other people's goods?

Do I live an overly materialistic life?

Have I accumulated excessive debt or failed to pay my debt?

The Covenant on the Mercy of God

"I will receive the Sacrament of Reconciliation once each month or immediately upon committing a serious sin. I will manifest the merciful Father by helping my family avoid the occasions of sin and performing one gratuitous act for each member of my family each week."

How fitting that the final covenant of TMIY is the covenant on mercy! Mercy underlies every covenant of TMIY. Mercy is the glue that binds them together. Mercy is the animating power within them.

The That Man is You! program begins with the story of King David. It is the story of a man blessed abundantly by God. It is the story of a man who falls into grievous sin and experiences dire consequences. Nonetheless, the story of King David is a story of hope for King David trusts in the mercy of God. When he encounters the mercy of God, King David becomes the only man in Scripture to be called "a man after God's heart" *(Acts 13:22)*.

The story of King David is our story. Many of us have fallen. We are in need of the mercy of God. We are in need of David's trust in the mercy of God: "Create in me a clean heart, O God, and put a new and right spirit within me. Cast me not away from thy presence, and take not thy holy Spirit from me. Restore to me the joy of thy salvation and uphold me with a willing spirit" *(Psalm 51:10ff)*.

That Man is You! exists so that men may encounter the mercy of God. Wherever you are in your spiritual life, Jesus Christ wants to encounter you right there and help take you to a better place. Once you have encountered the mercy of God, you will sing his praises and you will be merciful to those you meet.

Praised be the God whose mercy transcends the norms of his justice.

The Praise of God's Mercy

- Receive God's mercy in the Sacrament of Reconciliation. (preferably during Holy Week)

- Ask forgiveness of your wife and children for the times you haven't lived up to your high calling of husband and father.

- Receive the Eucharist on Easter morning.

- Recite the *Magnificat of Mary* in praise of the mercy of God. (see below)

- Celebrate with family and friends!

The Magnificat of Mary (Luke 1:46-55)

My soul doth magnify the Lord,

And my spirit hath rejoiced in God my Savior.

Because he hath regarded the humility of his handmaid;

For behold from henceforth all generations shall call me blessed.

Because he that is mighty, hath done great things to me; and holy is his name.

And his mercy is from generation unto generations, to them that fear him.

He hath showed might in his arm;

He hath scattered the proud in the conceit of their heart.

He hath put down the mighty from their seat,

And hath exalted the humble.

He hath filled the hungry with good things;

And the rich he hath sent empty away.

He hath received Israel his servant, being mindful of his mercy:

As he spoke to our fathers, to Abraham and to his seed forever.

The Seven Covenants of That Man is You!

❧ **The Covenant on Sexual Purity**
"I will live in sexual purity according to the sixth and ninth commandments and I will take whatever action is necessary to safeguard sexual purity for myself, my spouse and my children."

❧ **The Covenant on Financial Responsibility**
"I will become financially responsible for myself and my family by giving God the first fruits of my labor, saving a portion of my earnings and eliminating all credit card debt."

❧ **The Covenant on Reclaiming the Sabbath**
"I will reclaim Sunday as the Lord's Day by attending Mass together with my family and making the gift of that day to my family so that we may experience the superabundant joy of God together."

❧ **The Covenant on the Ascent of the Mind to God**
"I will elevate my mind to God by spending at least fifteen minutes each day gently reading Scripture and allowing God to speak to me. I will validate my insights through my spouse and/or my spiritual guide as appropriate."

❧ **The Covenant on Finding the Hidden Face of God**
"I will stop what I am doing and praise God seven times each day for discovering his Hidden Face in those closest to me, especially in my wife and children."

❧ **The Covenant on the Practice of the Presence of God**
"I will Practice the Presence of God by receiving Christ in the Eucharist one time each week in addition to Sunday. If I am unable to receive Him in the Eucharist, I will at least stop to visit Him residing in the Tabernacle."

❧ **The Covenant on the Mercy of God**
"I will receive the Sacrament of Reconciliation once each month or immediately upon committing a serious sin. I will manifest the merciful Father by helping my family avoid the occasions of sin and performing one gratuitous act for each member of my family each week."

The Path to Life

"I have set before you life and death, blessing and curse: therefore choose life, that you and your descendants may live." *(Deuteronomy 30:19ff)*

Great spiritual programs, fruitful Lenten journeys and moments of spiritual insight are blessings from God. They are to be preferred to all the treasures of this earth. Nonetheless, they are but seeds planted by God which we are called to cultivate so that they may grow and bear the fruit of holiness. This life of holiness is nothing other than a life of intimate union with God experienced within the context of our everyday lives, especially within the context of our marriages and family lives.

The Seven Covenants of That Man is You! provide the spiritual practices to till the soil, water the seed and prune the vine. They provide the means to overcome the obstacles in the spiritual life and open ourselves to an encounter with God. They provide the means to be immersed in God. They are a sure pathway to life.

Unfortunately, the Scriptures are full of stories of men who encounter and briefly follow God, only to later turn away. They fail to cultivate the seed that is planted. Instead, they allow the devil to snatch away that which was planted in their hearts. They allow the cares and anxieties of the world to drown out the still, small voice of God. They allow the desires of the flesh to turn them from their spiritual practices. They are in danger of becoming branches to be pruned: "If a man does not abide in me, he is cast forth as a branch and withers; and the branches are gathered, thrown into the fire and burned" *(John 15:6)*.

Contained in every encounter with God are a gift and a choice. The gift is mercy. Wherever you are in your spiritual life, Jesus Christ wants to encounter you right there and take you to a better place. He wants to take you to his Father's house. He wants to introduce you into communion with the Father so that you may experience superabundant joy. However, he will never force the encounter. He will never force the gift of mercy. The choice is yours.

Become a man after God's own heart!

Daily Plan of Lenten Journey

1. **MORNING CONSECRATION:** "Lord I trust in you with all my heart and I will not rely on my own intelligence. Help me to remember you in all my ways so that you may make straight my path. Amen."

2. **DAILY EXERCISE:** Spend 15 minutes each morning on the exercise indicated for each of the weeks of Lent.

3. **DAILY SACRIFICE OR OFFERING**

4. **NIGHT PRAYER**
   a. Briefly consider how you fulfilled your Lenten plan during the day and ask for the grace to fulfill it tomorrow.
   b. Close: "Lord, I trust in you with all my heart and I will not rely on my own intelligence. Help me to remember you in all my ways so that you may make straight my path. Amen."

THE MISERERE OF DAVID · Psalm 51

Have mercy on me, O God, according to thy great mercy.
And according to the multitude of thy tender mercies blot out my iniquity.
Wash me yet more from my iniquity, and cleanse me from my sin.
For I know my iniquity, and my sin is always before me.
To thee only have I sinned, and have done evil before thee: that thou mayst be justified in thy words, and mayst overcome when thou art judged.
For behold I was conceived in iniquities; and in sins did my mother conceive me.
For behold thou hast loved truth: the uncertain and hidden things of thy wisdom thou hast made manifest to me.
Thou shalt sprinkle me with hyssop, and I shall be cleansed: thou shalt wash me, and I shall be made whiter than snow.
To my hearing thou shalt give joy and gladness: and the bones that have been humbled shall rejoice.
Turn away thy face from my sins, and blot out all my iniquities.
Create a clean heart in me, O God: and renew a right spirit within my bowels.
Cast me not away from thy face; and take not thy holy spirit from me.
Restore unto me the joy of thy salvation, and strengthen me with a perfect spirit.
I will teach the unjust thy ways: and the wicked shall be converted to thee.
Deliver me from blood, O God, thou God of my salvation: and my tongue shall extol thy justice.
O Lord, thou wilt open my lips: and my mouth shall declare thy praise.
For if thou hadst desired sacrifice, I would indeed have given it: with burnt offerings thou wilt not be delighted.
A sacrifice to God is an afflicted spirit: a contrite and humbled heart, O God, thou wilt not despise.
Deal favourably, O Lord, in thy good will with Zion; that the walls of Jerusalem may be built up.
Then shalt thou accept the sacrifice of justice, oblations and whole burnt offerings: then shall they lay calves upon thy altar.

The Seven Daily Praises of God

PRAISE UPON RISING

"O Lord God of hosts, how lovely is your dwelling place! One day within your courts is better than a thousand elsewhere. I would rather be a doorkeeper in the house of the Lord than to dwell in the tents of the wicked. Blessed are those who dwell in your house forever singing your praises."

MORNING PRAISE

"O merciful Father, what is man that you should mindful of him, mortal man that you should care for him? Yet to ransom a sinner you gave away your only beloved Son. How great is your name, O Lord our God, through all the earth!"

MIDMORNING PRAISE

"O beloved Son of the Father, in your light we see light. We behold the revelation of the Father, slow to anger and abiding in compassion. O Lord, your mercy is as high as the heavens and as deep as the nether world. How great is your name, O Lord our God, through all the earth!"

MIDDAY PRAISE

"O Spirit of love, you transform us from glory unto glory into the image of the only begotten of the Father. What you reveal to us now dimly as in a mirror, you will one day reveal to us face to face. How great is your name, O Lord our God, through all the earth!"

MIDAFTERNOON PRAISE

"O mystery of life and love, how sweet the path of those who find you abiding in their homes, who gaze upon the beauty of your face and hear the sweet sound of your voice. Praise to you, Lord of heaven and earth, for you have hidden these things from the wise and learned and have revealed them to the pure of heart."

EVENING PRAISE

"O Emmanuel! How great your love for those who serve you! How near your presence to those who love you! You dwell with those gathered in your name. Stay with us, Lord, for the day is far spent and evening presses. O Emmanuel, be ever near to us!"

NIGHT PRAISE

"O gracious God, now you may let your servant go in peace for your word has been fulfilled; my own eyes have beheld your mercy that is from generation unto generation to those who love you. How great is your name, O Lord our God, through all the earth!"

Made in the USA
Columbia, SC
25 January 2024